CLOSER LOOK AT

KT-433-572

ACID RAIN

Alex Edmonds

Franklin Watts
LONDON ● SYDNEY

© Aladdin Books Ltd 1996
Designed and produced by
Aladdin Books Ltd
28 Percy Street
London W1P 0LD

First published in Great Britain
in 1996 by
Franklin Watts
96 Leonard Street
London EC2A 4RH

A catalogue record for this book is available from the British Library.

ISBN: 0 7496 2454 X (hb)
ISBN: 0 7496 3559 2 (pb)

Editor
Selina Wood
Designer
Gary Edgar-Hyde
Picture Research
Brooks Krikler Research
Front cover design
Karen Lieberman
Illustrators
Ron Hayward Associates
David Burroughs
Biz Hill
Ian Moores
Mike Saunders
Banjo Illustration

Certain illustrations have appeared in
earlier books created by Aladdin Books.

Consultants
Sue Hare and Jane McNairn are researchers at the
Atmospheric Research and Information Centre,
Manchester Metropolitan University

Printed in Belgium

CONTENTS

INTRODUCTION

Rain is an essential ingredient for life. The water provided by rain allows all life on Earth to survive. It waters our crops, allowing us to grow food for us to eat and food for the animals we raise for meat and milk. Although rain is naturally acidic, it is being increasingly acidified by pollution from our homes, factories, power stations and cars. The term used to describe this problem is "acid rain".

ubstances called acids have a sharp taste known as acidity. Ordinary rain-water is slightly acidic. But in severely polluted areas, rain can be as acidic as the acids lemon juice or vinegar. Rain which is very acidic can cause damage to trees, lakes, wildlife, buildings and human health.

Is acid rain wet?

The term "acid rain" (or acid deposition) does not fully describe what it is, as acid rain is not always wet. The term includes acid snow, hail, mist and fog, as well as a dry, invisible dust. All these types of acid rain introduce harmful acids into the environment. The photo (above) shows dry acid rain pollution in Paris; below, we see wet acid rain.

WHAT IS

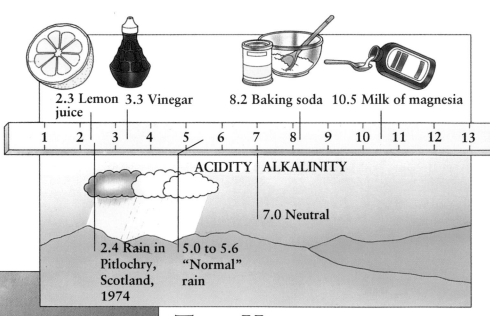

2.3 Lemon juice   3.3 Vinegar   8.2 Baking soda   10.5 Milk of magnesia

1   2   3   4   5   6   7   8   9   10   11   12   13   14

ACIDITY | ALKALINITY

7.0 Neutral

2.4 Rain in Pitlochry, Scotland, 1974

5.0 to 5.6 "Normal" rain

THE pH SCALE

The pH scale is used for measuring the acid or alkali in a substance. Alkali is the opposite of acid. Milk of magnesia (medicine for an upset stomach) is an alkali. The lower the number, the higher the amount of acid. Some acids are poisonous, some are harmless. Rain below pH 5.0 is said to be "acid rain".

ON CLOSER INSPECTION
– *What is rain?*

When liquid water is heated by the Sun, it evaporates to form water vapour in the air. Then this air, which is warm and full of moisture, rises into the atmosphere, cooling as it moves upwards. This turns the moisture into liquid again, which then falls as drops of rain.

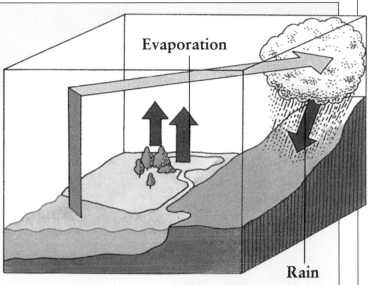

Evaporation

Rain

ACID RAIN?

Key

Oxides of sulphur

Oxides of nitrogen

Moisture (H_2O)

Nitric acid

Sulphuric acid

HOW ACID RAIN FORMS

This diagram shows one way in which acid rain is formed. Two of the major ingredients of acid rain are the chemicals sulphur dioxide (SO_2) and nitrogen oxides (NO_x). When large quantities of these two particular chemicals enter the atmosphere, they team up with moisture (H_2O) to produce strong acids – sulphuric acid and nitric acid. These two acids, which are formed in the atmosphere, are very strong pollutants (substances that can cause harm to the environment).

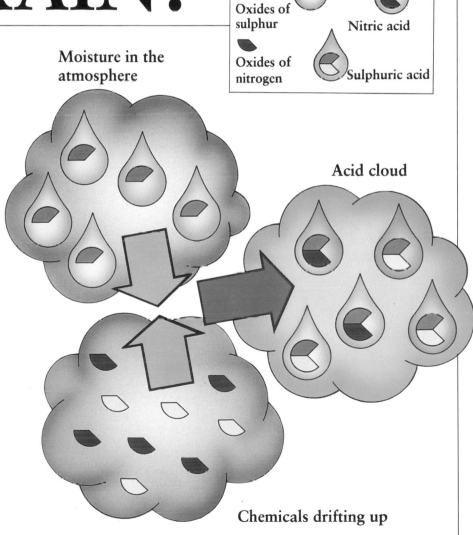

Moisture in the atmosphere

Acid cloud

Chemicals drifting up

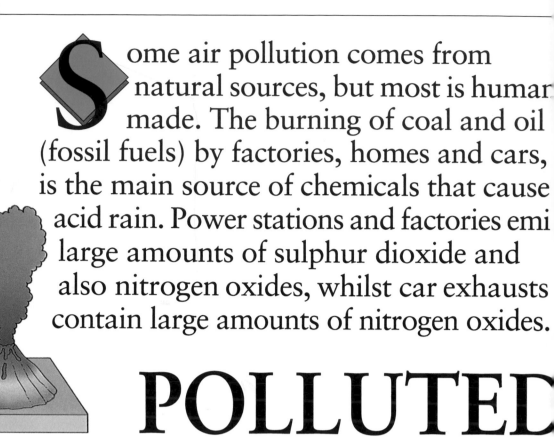

Some air pollution comes from natural sources, but most is human made. The burning of coal and oil (fossil fuels) by factories, homes and cars, is the main source of chemicals that cause acid rain. Power stations and factories emit large amounts of sulphur dioxide and also nitrogen oxides, whilst car exhausts contain large amounts of nitrogen oxides.

POLLUTED

Unnatural 90%	Natural 10 %

SO_2 sources

Normally, about half of the SO_2 in the atmosphere is natural. It is produced by erupting volcanoes, swamps, forest fires and animal and plant decay. The rest of the SO_2 pollution is human-made. In some industrial regions, the human-made SO_2 in the air can be as high as 90% (see above).

ACID RAIN IN ACTION

Once acid pollution is emitted into the atmosphere, some of it falls to the ground close to where it was produced, as dry deposition. The remainder is carried into the sky, where it mixes with water vapour, sunlight and oxygen to form sulphuric and nitric acid. These are carried by the wind over distances and at some point fall as acid rain or snow.

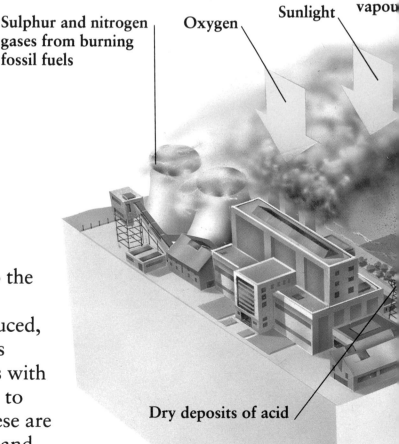

Sulphur and nitrogen gases from burning fossil fuels

Oxygen

Sunlight

Water vapou

Dry deposits of acid

On Closer Inspection
– *Volcanic SO₂*

When volcanoes erupt, they emit various gases which have been trapped under the ground, including sulphur dioxide. This can cause air pollution, which can then be made much worse by the addition of human-made emissions.

SKIES

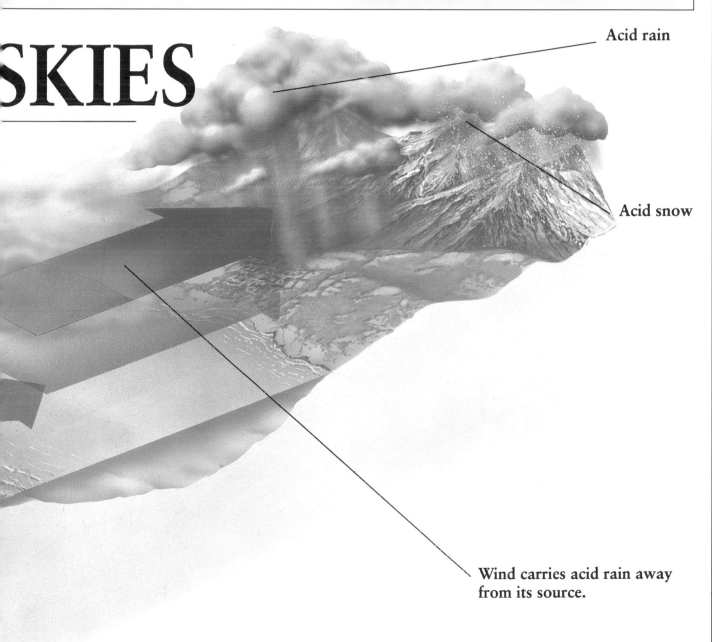

Acid rain

Acid snow

Wind carries acid rain away from its source.

cid rain has been an issue for several hundred years, ever since people noticed that smoke from chimneys was unpleasant to breathe in. Last century people realised that the smoke pumped out from factories and homes was falling back to Earth as coloured rain.

THE CULPRITS

Oil
The Middle East and South America hold over 60% of the world's oil, but it is high-sulphur oil. Oil containing low amounts of sulphur is expensive, but is less polluting. As world fossil fuels such as oil start to run out, we will need to find alternatives.

AN INDUSTRIAL PROBLEM

The majority of combined SO_2 and NO_x pollution comes from industrial processes. Power stations, in particular, emit huge amounts of SO_2. The smelting process (extraction of metals from metal ores by heating) and oil refineries also produce much SO_2. The burning of fossil fuels in industry produces 91 million tonnes of combined SO_2 and NO_x worldwide, every year.

Car emissions
Exhaust fumes (left) are full of poisonous gases. Road traffic is expected to double by 2010 in western Europe. This would mean an increase in nitrogen oxides from traffic emissions.

ON CLOSER INSPECTION
– *A murky past*

In 1852, Robert Smith, a chemist, found rainfall in Manchester, U.K., to be very acidic. He suggested a link between acid rain and SO_2 given off when coal was burned by local factories. His was the first indication, over 100 years ago!

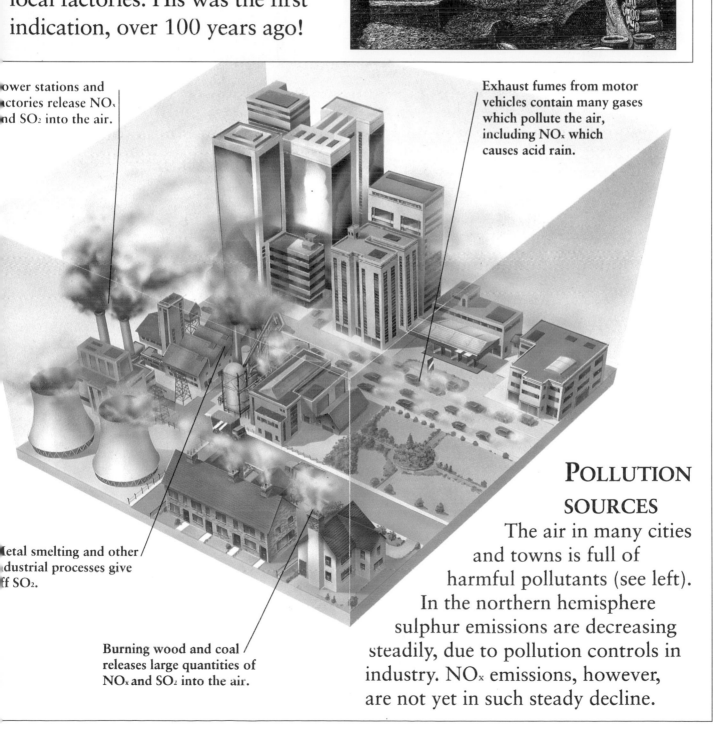

ower stations and actories release NO_x and SO_2 into the air.

Exhaust fumes from motor vehicles contain many gases which pollute the air, including NO_x which causes acid rain.

Metal smelting and other industrial processes give off SO_2.

Burning wood and coal releases large quantities of NO_x and SO_2 into the air.

POLLUTION
SOURCES

The air in many cities and towns is full of harmful pollutants (see left). In the northern hemisphere sulphur emissions are decreasing steadily, due to pollution controls in industry. NO_x emissions, however, are not yet in such steady decline.

Once acid rain is formed, it can stay up in the clouds for a long time. These clouds can be carried off by the wind to other areas, sometimes hundreds of kilometres away, where they eventually fall to Earth as acid rain or snow. This is called transboundary pollution.

WORLDWIDE

SCANDINAVIAN PROBLEM

Winds sweep millions of tonnes of sulphur, poured into the air from factories, towards Scandinavia (below). When it comes down to Earth as sulphuric acid, it has an acidifying effect on soil and water in the area.

TALL CHIMNEYS

The effects of air pollution used to be greatest around where it was produced. So, many countries built high smoke stacks to send chemicals out of harm's way (above). But all this did was push the emissions higher into the air, where they remain longer and travel further.

ON CLOSER INSPECTION
– *Pollutants on the move*

How far emissions travel and how acidic they are depend on weather conditions – wind, cloud cover, humidity and sunlight. They are also affected by the height at which the pollutants are released, which depends on the chimney height.

PROBLEMS

MEXICAN TRADE

On the border between Mexico and the U.S.A., winds create a "trade" in pollution. At night, they blow south, carrying chemicals from the U.S.A. into Mexico. Then during the day, the winds blow north, carrying them back again. As a result, both countries suffer acidifying damage (see below).

A MAJOR CULPRIT

Britain, Germany and Poland especially are homes to polluting industries. British emissions not only generate nearly 90% of Britain's acid deposition, but they are also swept by winds to Scandinavia, where they fall as acid rain.

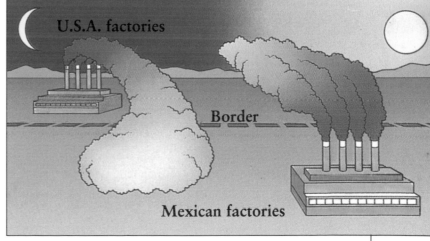

U.S.A. factories

Border

Mexican factories

All over Europe and North America, previously healthy forests are dead or dying – probably the result of acid rain. Trees were damaged at an alarming pace during the mid-1980s – by the end of the decade more than half of the trees in Germany were showing signs of acid damage.

Forest damage
In western Germany, the percentage of trees damaged by acid rain rose from 8% to 50% in six years (left).

1982	1983	1988
8%	34%	52%

FOREST

WHAT ARE TREES WORTH?

Scandinavian forests (right) are a major source of wood-based products (such as furniture and wood pulp). They are very important to Scandinavian countries; if forests are destroyed, it will effect the livelihoods of loggers (below).

ON CLOSER INSPECTION
– Wildlife at risk

Forest floors that are affected by acid have high concentrations of metals like aluminium and lead. When animals (right) drink from acidic lakes and dew that has been affected, the metals can build up in their kidneys and livers, and gradually poison them.

DEATHS

HOW TREES ARE DAMAGED

The acid from rain takes important minerals from the leaves of the trees and from the soil. Acid rain also releases toxic metals from the soil which damage the roots of the trees. Trees are weakened, cannot grow properly and are attacked by viruses, fungi and pests. The trees then suffer from stunted growth and often lose their needles or leaves. Eventually the trees may die. Direct damage to trees occurs when SO_2 blocks the pores on the leaves, through which the trees takes in the air they need to live. Another symptom of acid damage is "panic shoots". These occur when trees affected by acid rain lose their leaves and produce short branches to replace them.

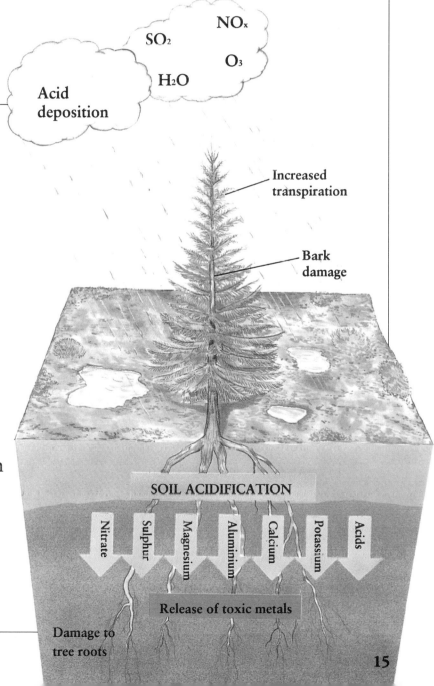

Acid deposition

SO_2 NO_x O_3 H_2O

Increased transpiration

Bark damage

SOIL ACIDIFICATION

Nitrate Sulphur Magnesium Aluminium Calcium Potassium Acids

Release of toxic metals

Damage to tree roots

15

Clear problem

Acidified lakes are beautifully clear, due, in part, to the death of plankton (below). These tiny plants give healthy lakes a muddyish tinge, but they are early victims of acidity.

A lake that has been polluted by acid rain looks clean and crystal clear, but contains hardly any life. A healthy lake has a pH of around 6.5 and all kinds of plants, insects and fish live there. Once the pH drops below 6.0, species begin to die out as the lake starts to acidify. All over the world lakes are affected.

ACID

Crayfish

Crayfish (below) and shrimps are some of the first victims of an acidified lake. When the pH level drops to just below 6.0, crayfish and some types of mayfly begin to die out. Lakes with a pH of less than 5.0 are unlikely to contain any fish.

OTHER POTENTIAL PROBLEMS

Of Sweden's 90,000 lakes, 40,000 are known to be affected by acid (below). In the U.S.A., one in five lakes are thought to be seriously acidified. Acid rain can fall directly onto lakes, or can drain into them from hills. Also, aluminium metal is washed out of acidified soil into lakes. Only water beetles and worms can survive happily in these conditions.

ON CLOSER INSPECTION
– Grave problems

Most sensitive to acid are lichens (on the gravestone, right) and mosses, because their leaves have no protective coating. They are often used as indicators of SO₂ air pollution. In polluted towns, lichens may be completely absent.

LAKES

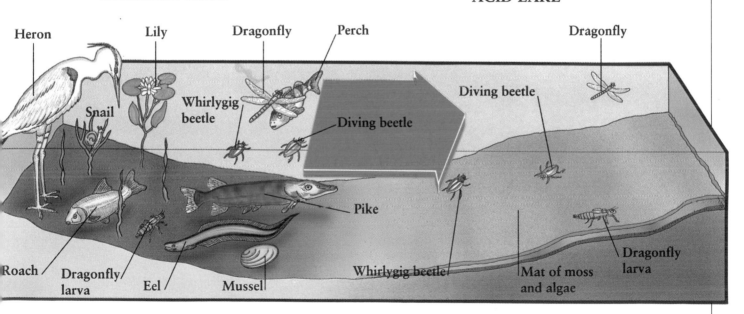

HEALTHY LAKE   **ACID LAKE**

Heron · Lily · Dragonfly · Perch · Dragonfly · Whirlygig beetle · Diving beetle · Diving beetle · Snail · Pike · Roach · Dragonfly larva · Eel · Mussel · Whirlygig beetle · Mat of moss and algae · Dragonfly larva

THE DEATH OF A LAKE

The diagram above shows how the cycle of life around a lake is affected by acid rain. When tiny plants and insects die, fish also die off, which removes the main food source for birds. Birds are also at risk from poisonous metals (such as aluminium, zinc and lead) washed into the lake. These metals are absorbed by insect larvae, which birds eat. Over time, a lake polluted by acid supports only the most resistant species.

oft building stones, such as limestone and sandstone, have always suffered from erosion by the natural elements of wind and rain. There is evidence now that buildings in, or near a large city or industrial area are at risk from high levels of acid rain.

CORROSION

Acid glass

Some stained-glass windows are 1,000 years old, but in the last 30 years acid damage has become a problem. Blackening of pale colours in the glass (see the man's face in the window above) is a common result of acid rain. Windows may be restored (below).

On Closer Inspection
– *Natural erosion*

Rain and wind have always caused the natural weathering of rocks. Spider Mountain (right) in Arizona, U.S.A., is an example of dramatic natural weathering of sandstone. The soft outer layer of sandstone has weathered away, leaving the harder rock sculpted in an unusual shape.

BUILDINGS AT RISK

Acid pollution spoils the colour of paint, weakens leather and erodes building materials. Sulphur pollutants react with minerals in limestone to form a powdery substance, which is then washed away by rain (left). Below, we see black gypsum caused by acid rain, formed on limestone in Venice. It later blisters off, leaving the stone unprotected.

OUR HERITAGE

Many of the world's famous buildings are at risk from acid pollution. Damage to the beautiful Taj Mahal in India (below), caused by sulphur pollution from nearby oil refineries, was one of the first indicators of acid pollution occurring in the developing world.

There is a link between acid rain and damage to human health. People can be harmed by breathing in the chemicals from dry deposition, causing chest illnesses. Also, when acid rain causes the release of chemicals and metals into drinking water, it can damage people's health.

Protect yourself
In many cities where air pollution is a problem, people who spend a lot of time outside, such as cyclists, wear anti-pollution masks to filter out the pollutants from the air they breathe (above).

CHOKING ON "FRESH" AIR

When air pollution is breathed in as people walk along the street, it gets into their lungs. Once in the lungs, it acts like a poison, causing the airways in the respiratory system to get narrower. This lets in less oxygen and breathing becomes difficult. It also puts stress on the heart. If SO_2 is breathed in, it can pass deep into the alveoli, which is where oxygen is passed into the blood. The moisture in the lungs can turn the sulphur dioxide into sulphuric acid, and cause damage to the body.

HUMAN

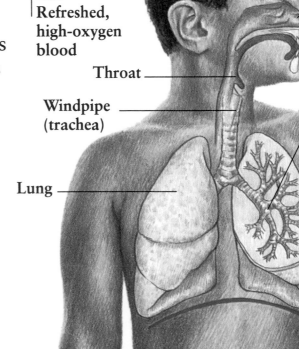

Alveoli

Stale, low-oxygen blood on its way to absorb more oxygen

Refreshed, high-oxygen blood

Nasal passag

Throat

Windpipe (trachea)

Bronch

Lung

ON CLOSER INSPECTION
– *Smog check*

In some polluted cities, such as those in California, U.S.A., smog check stations have been set up to monitor the output of polluting exhaust gases, and to take cars off the road until they are fixed.

HEALTH

CONTAMINATED WATER

In Norway and Sweden, many people get their drinking water directly from wells (below). Aluminium pollution can be washed into the water supply by acid rain and this has been linked to cases of kidney failure in people in Norway.

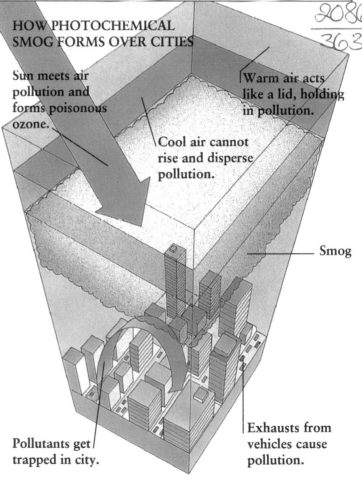

HOW PHOTOCHEMICAL SMOG FORMS OVER CITIES

Sun meets air pollution and forms poisonous ozone.

Warm air acts like a lid, holding in pollution.

Cool air cannot rise and disperse pollution.

Smog

Pollutants get trapped in city.

Exhausts from vehicles cause pollution.

PHOTOCHEMICAL SMOG

Photochemical smog (smoky fog) occurs in big cities when sunlight meets nitrogen oxides from car exhausts and other pollutants. This forms the poisonous gas ozone. This smog causes eye irritation and breathing problems and has been linked with cancer.

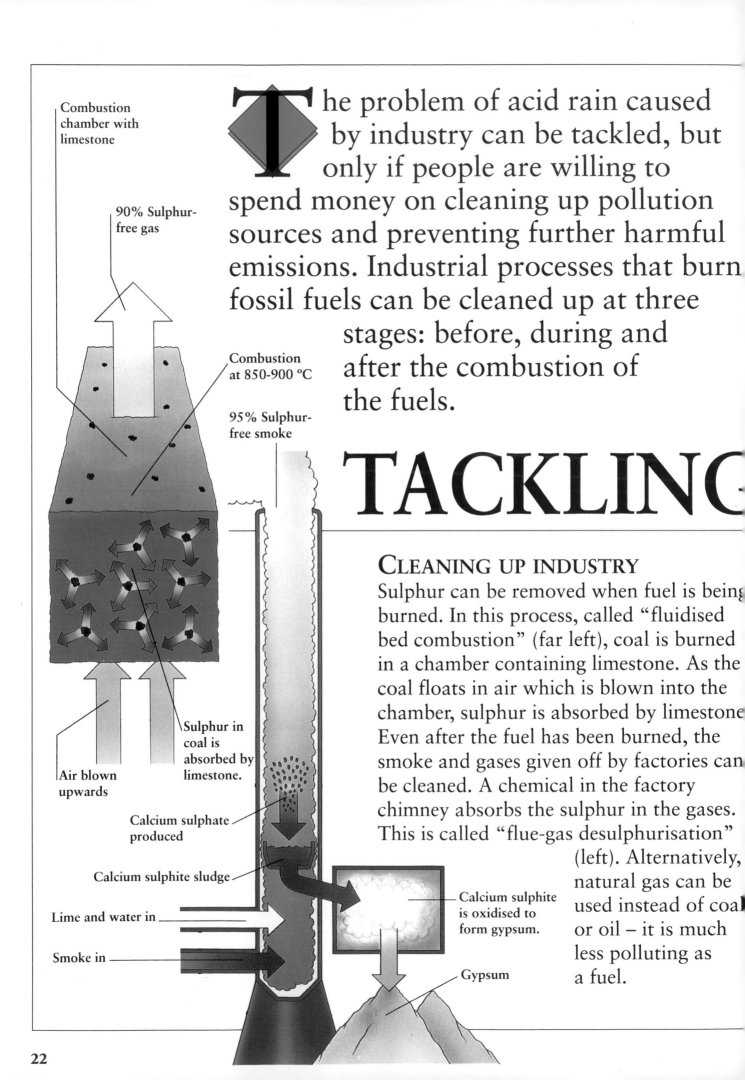

Combustion chamber with limestone

90% Sulphur-free gas

Combustion at 850-900 °C

95% Sulphur-free smoke

Sulphur in coal is absorbed by limestone.

Air blown upwards

Calcium sulphate produced

Calcium sulphite sludge

Lime and water in

Smoke in

Calcium sulphite is oxidised to form gypsum.

Gypsum

The problem of acid rain caused by industry can be tackled, but only if people are willing to spend money on cleaning up pollution sources and preventing further harmful emissions. Industrial processes that burn fossil fuels can be cleaned up at three stages: before, during and after the combustion of the fuels.

TACKLING

CLEANING UP INDUSTRY

Sulphur can be removed when fuel is being burned. In this process, called "fluidised bed combustion" (far left), coal is burned in a chamber containing limestone. As the coal floats in air which is blown into the chamber, sulphur is absorbed by limestone. Even after the fuel has been burned, the smoke and gases given off by factories can be cleaned. A chemical in the factory chimney absorbs the sulphur in the gases. This is called "flue-gas desulphurisation" (left). Alternatively, natural gas can be used instead of coal or oil – it is much less polluting as a fuel.

ON CLOSER INSPECTION
– Gulf oil pollution

During the Gulf War of 1991, hundreds of Kuwaiti oil wells were set alight. The result was an extreme example of what burning fossil fuels does to the environment. The smoke, which contained vast amounts of poisonous gases, plunged Kuwait into darkness during the daytime.

THE PROBLEM

FUTURE POWER

In the Akou power plant in Japan (right), expensive cleaning devices, called scrubbers, are fitted around the chimneys as part of a flue-gas desulphurisation system. Emissions pass through the chimneys and are sprayed with a mixture of limestone and H_2O. This removes SO_2 emissions by up to 90%. Many other countries, however, find this, and other cleaning processes, too expensive to introduce.

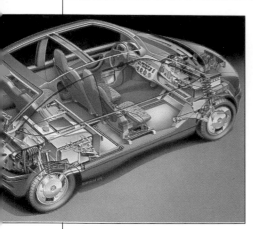

There are some ways of combating the effects of acidification, however, the best way to solve the problem is to prevent emissions of pollutants in the first place. Reducing the amount of NO_x emissions caused by car exhaust is an effective solution.

MORE CLEA

A first step
Electric cars powered by battery packs, instead of by engines that burn oil, are being developed. But fossil fuels are still needed to produce the electricity that charges the batteries.

CAR CONTROL
In developing areas like Eastern Europe, Asia and Africa, where car buying is increasing (below), there is little money to introduce pollution controls. NO_x pollution is likely to increase drastically as a result.

IMMEDIATE ACTION
There is a short-term method of controlling acidity in lakes – tonnes of lime can be poured over the lake. This neutralises the acidity because lime is alkaline – the opposite of acid. However, this process is difficult to implement, is expensive and has to be repeated every 4 to 5 years (above).

ON CLOSER INSPECTION – Slow down!

Cars produce the least amount of pollution when they are driven steadily on long journeys (right), because hot engines burn fuel more efficiently. Short trips, even at low speeds, produce lots of emissions.

REDUCE SPEED NOW

NING UP

AKE THE TRAIN

ublic transport systems need to be nproved so that people can travel vithout having to use their cars. If more eople used public transport, it would ut the number of private vehicles on the oads, and would thus reduce pollution.

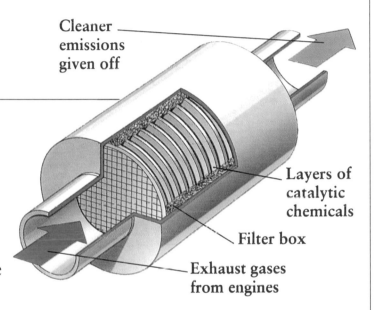

Cleaner emissions given off

Layers of catalytic chemicals

Filter box

Exhaust gases from engines

Catalytic converter

A catalytic converter (above) is a special chamber which can be fitted to the exhaust system of a car. It alters poisonous fumes from the car engine, making them harmless, and can cut harmful nitrogen oxide emissions by up to 90%. Today, cars sold in the European Union have to have them fitted, as do cars in the U.S.A.

25

Acid pollution is no longer a local problem. It must be tackled globally. Industrialised countries are taking measures to clean the air, with many governments demanding that industry cleans up its act. As industry grows in developing countries, acid rain will become a major problem if governments do not introduce controls on emissions.

Global action
In 1985, the first sulphur protocol, signed by 20 countries, required them to reduce SO_2 emissions by 30% by 1993. They achieved this, and are now working to reduce SO_2 by 50% by 2000.

LIMITS TO

DEVELOPING PROBLEMS
Power stations in developing countries use brown coal. It is cheaper than hard coal, but much dirtier when it is burned. Another problem is that many of these countries have old, inefficient industrial equipment. They also have fewer safety controls, so produce dirtier emissions.

DIFFERENT SOLUTIONS
In the future we may see the introduction of controls like those in Athens, Greece (above). When pollution from cars is at its worst in Athens, all cars are banned from the city centre.

ON CLOSER INSPECTION – *Air check*

Air management schemes, like this one in Los Angeles, U.S.A., have been introduced in many cities. The glass suction tube takes in air samples for analysis of air quality. Perhaps in the future these will be introduced in all cities with a high number of cars, and in industrial areas.

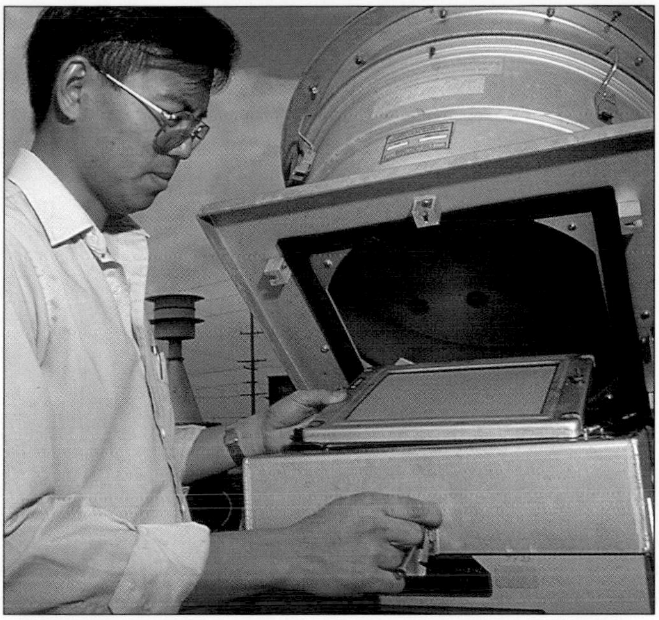

PROGRESS

ˉHE FUTURE

ossil fuel reserves are spread unevenly round the world. As oil, gas and coal ın out, prices will rise nd developing ountries will find it ifficult to afford xpensive ollution controls. ome people rgue that we ıould leave coal nd oil deposits nder the ground. Ve could then oncentrate research into further nergy resources, especially ıose that are renewable.

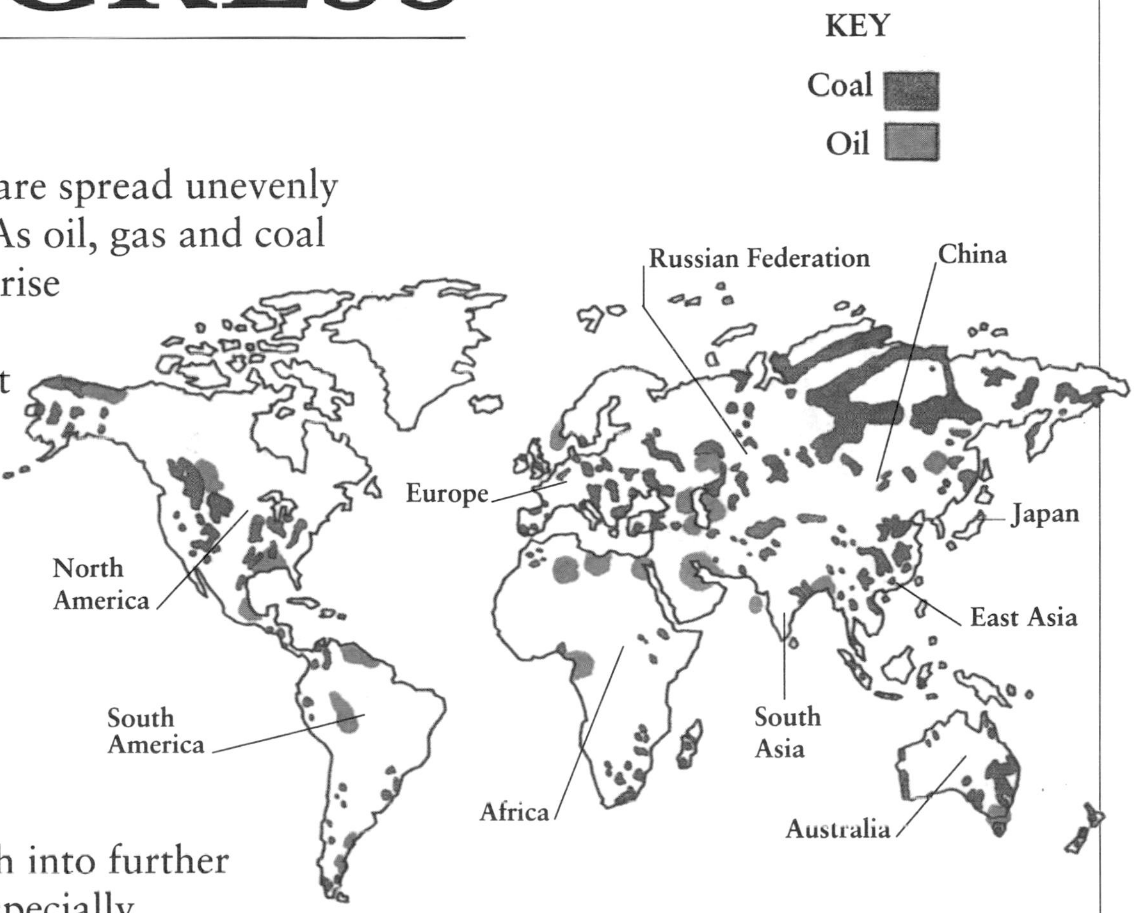
KEY
Coal
Oil
Russian Federation
China
Europe
Japan
North America
East Asia
South America
South Asia
Africa
Australia

WORLD ENERGY RESOURCES

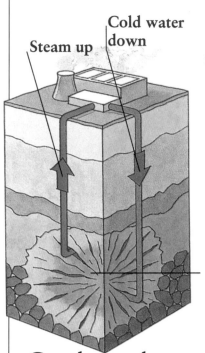

Steam up

Cold water down

Cracks through hot rocks

Geothermal power

Deep in the Earth's core it is extremely hot (4,000-4,500 °C). In some places these hot rocks can be reached by boring holes. Heat energy in the form of steam can be extracted for many years before the rocks cool down (above).

SOLAR POWER

Solar power harnesses the Sun's energy and can be used in two ways. Solar panels on the roofs of buildings absorb radiation from the Sun, which is used for heating homes. Solar cells at solar power stations (right) use the Sun's light, not heat, to generate electricity for various purposes. Solar power works best in regions which are sunny all year round.

Concern for the welfare of the planet is growing. New ideas for tackling pollution are constantly put forward, including a tax on energy sources that pollute. But the best long-term solution is to find energy sources that cause little or no air pollution when used, and that are renewable.

NEW ENERGY

On Closer Inspection
– *A new way of life?*

The Centre for Alternative Technology in Wales promotes new technologies that could be developed to provide energy. In the photo we see the use of wind turbines. The wind turns the turbine blades, which drive generators that produce electricity.

SOURCES

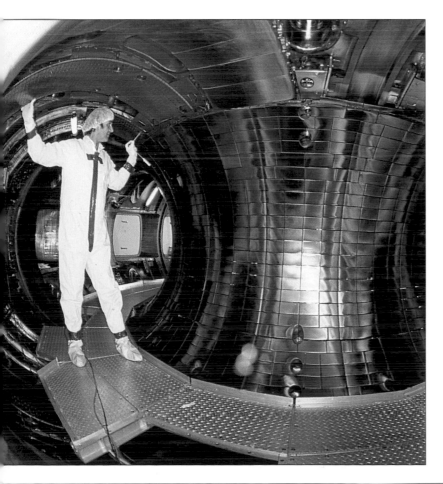

TOKAMAK

Scientists have discovered how to control nuclear fusion reactions, like those that power the Sun and the hydrogen bomb. This provides a renewable source of energy which is not polluting. The reaction, which takes place at very high temperatures, combines two forms of hydrogen and produces helium and a huge amount of energy. But at the moment, the energy produced is about the same amount as that which is needed to start the process.

The inside of the Tokamak Fusion Reactor in New Jersey, U.S.A.

FRIENDS *of the* earth

GREENPEACE

GET INFORMED

An important thing we can all do is make people aware of problems cause by acid rain. Get information from newspapers, environmental groups an A.R.I.C., then you'll always be able to tell people about the threat of acid rai

WHAT CAN YOU DO?

HOW TO TRAVEL

Cut back on car use – walk to school or go by bicycle or public transport. If you have to use a car in your family always try to carry more than one person in the car. Just one person travelling in a car is a waste of energy.

RECYCLING

Many materials such as paper (right), can be recycled and used again. Energy can be saved, provided that recycling uses less energy than the original production process. Each year, British homes throw away about 18 million tonnes of rubbish. 80% of this could be recycled!

TO SUM IT ALL UP...

In most of the industrialised world, the air is cleaner now than it was 50 years ago. This is because methods of reducing pollution have slowly been put into action. The battle against acid rain has begun, but we must continue to pressurise governments to tackle acid rain and banish it forever.

Acid A sharp, sour substance that can erode other substances and that has a pH of less than on the pH scale.

Acid deposition Rain, snow, hail, fog and dust which is acidic as a result of acid pollution. Another name for acid rain.

Acid rain Rain, snow, hail and fog which is acidic as a result of pollution. The term also includes dry deposition.

Alveoli Tiny cells in the lungs where oxygen is absorbed by blood and carbon dioxide taken out of the blood.

Atmosphere The layer of gases that surrounds the Earth. It contains the gases oxygen, nitrogen, carbon dioxide and water vapour.

Catalytic Using a catalyst (a substance that speeds up a chemical reaction).

Combustion Burning.

Dry deposition Gases and particles of acid pollution in the atmosphere, most of which fall locally.

Emissions Substances like gases that are released (emitted) into the environment.

Evaporation The process by which a substance changes into a state of vapour.

Fossil fuel A fuel such as coal, natural gas or oil, which is formed over millions of years from decaying plants and animals.

Geothermal energy The heat energy stored in the Earth itself.

Gypsum A soft calcium mineral used in making cement and plasters.

Livelihood The way in which someone earns money to live and support themself.

Nuclear fusion The creation of a new nucleus from two lighter ones, producing a release of energy.

Nucleus The central mass of an atom.

Ozone A form of oxygen with three atoms; a bluish gas with a bitter smell. In the lower atmosphere it combines with nitrogen oxide to form photochemical smog.

Photochemical smog A form of air pollution caused by the action of the Sun's radiation on exhaust gases from cars and factories.

GLOSSARY

Photosynthesis The method plants use to convert the Sun's energy into sugars for growth.

Pollutant A substance that causes pollution.

Pollution Natural or human-made substances that harm the environment.

Respiratory system The system in the body that controls breathing.

Smelting The melting of metal ore to separate metal from ore.

Transboundary pollution The transportation of acid pollution by wind to areas a long way from the pollution's source.

Turbine A machine that converts the energy from a moving fluid or gas into another form of energy, such as electricity.

Vapour A substance in the form of mist, fumes or smoke.

INDEX